My Little TRUTHFUL TRUMPET

PETER PAUPER PRESS, INC.
Rye Brook, New York

PETER PAUPER PRESS

In 1928, at the age of twenty-two, Peter Beilenson began printing books on a small press in the basement of his parents' home in Larchmont, New York. Peter—and later, his wife, Edna—sought to create fine books that sold at "prices even a pauper could afford."

Today, still family owned and operated, Peter Pauper Press continues to honor our founders' legacy of quality, value, and fun for big kids and small kids alike.

Written by Hannah Beilenson
Designed by Heather Zschock

3 International Drive
Rye Brook, NY 10573 USA

Published in the UK and Europe by Peter Pauper Press, Inc.
c/o White Pebble International
Units 2-3, Spring Business Park
Stanbridge Road
Havant, Hampshire PO9 2GJ, UK

ISBN 978-1-4413-4209-6
Printed in China

7 6 5 4 3 2 1

OUR ACTIONS AND US

Have you ever tried something new? Shared a toy or snack? Given a hug or high five when someone needed it? Well, those are just a few examples of putting your feelings into action! And every action you take can make a change. You can make people smile and laugh, help others feel safe, and create something new for everyone to share. There's so much you can do, and there's no wrong place to start—so let's take action today!

One action is **Honesty**, and we'll meet someone who will help us learn more about it.

I love Mr. Johnson's band class!
Me, too! Especially the drums.

Oh, no! I broke a drumstick. What should I do?
Maybe you can hide it!
Or, you could tell the truth.

Who said that?
I did! I'm a Truthful Trumpet—
I can help you be honest.

I know I'm *supposed* to be honest, but what if I have a good reason to lie?
Yeah, we could get in trouble for breaking the drumstick!

Sometimes, you can get in trouble when you tell the truth.

But if you lie, someone else could get in trouble instead.

And if you tell the truth,
it lets people know
that they can trust you.
But what *is* trust?

Trust is when people can rely on you, and you can rely on them, too.

LIBRARY
It's when you keep
your promises,

give back things
that aren't yours to keep,

and when you tell the truth. People will know
they can trust you when you're honest.
What about little lies?
Like when I don't want
to hurt someone's feelings.

Sometimes you might want to lie to be nice,

Wow, you must have worked so hard on this!
but you don't have to lie to be kind—just say something that's true!

This can show people you care, even if you don't always like something.

I guess you're right, but I still don't want to get in trouble, or have Mr. Johnson be mad at me.

When honesty feels hard, just try to follow these three steps:

That's how you can learn from your mistakes and show that you care.

Mr. Johnson, I broke a drumstick. It was an accident, and I'm really sorry.

Why don't you help me fix it with some tape? Then it can be a practice drumstick.
Okay! And I'll make sure to be more careful from now on.

Thanks for helping me
tell the truth.
No problem! And now we can
get back to making music.

Meet My Truthful Trumpet

My Truthful Trumpet's name is:

....

I told the truth when I:

....

....

....

When honesty is hard, I try to:

....

....

....

....